HANOI
THE CITY AT A GLANCE

CW00558506

Hanoi Towers
A landmark building due to its height ₐₙd
it being a symbol of the reforming ecoₙₒₘy
of Vietnam, particularly as this hotel ₐₙd
apartment complex sits directly on top ₒf the
old 'Hanoi Hilton' prison, where the ghosts
of the past are contained in a museum.
See p068

Ba Dinh Square
By the West Lake, this is where you'll find the
colonial-era Presidential Palace and brutalist
mausoleum and museum of Ho Chi Minh, both
built under the supervision of Soviet architect
Garold Gregorievich Isakovitch.
See p010 and p027

West Lake
The shores of Ho Tay are home to Hanoi's
swankiest private residences and a clutch
of modern hotels and spas, built in between
all the temples and pagodas.

Old Quarter
The bustling lanes and narrow 'tube houses'
of this historic district are a mishmash of
periods and styles, but make for a fascinating
and atmospheric amble among the artisans.
See p028

St Joseph's Cathedral
The city's cathedral was built in 1886 during
the early colonial era. It boasts beautiful
stained-glass windows and dominates Nha
Tho and the surrounding area, which is full
of smart restaurants, bars and boutiques.
Nha Tho

INTRODUCTION
THE CHANGING FACE OF THE URBAN SCENE

Ho Chi Minh City may well have been quicker out of the starting blocks in embracing market liberalisation, but Hanoi, historically a one-party city rather than a Party City, is catching up fast. The new money from trade and tourism is flowing into renovated French colonial villas or courtyards in neighbourhoods such as the Old Quarter, which now houses chichi restaurants, designer boutiques and a flourishing contemporary art scene; the north of Vietnam was always the more traditional and cultured end of the country, the place with the first university, the lacquer links to China and the healing herbs of the hill peoples.

These days, for all its tiger-economy development, maddening traffic and dense crush of people, the city retains an intimate, manageable feel. You can gad about Hanoi's lakes and alleys, the Frenchified avenues and Soviet-era monuments on foot, slurping up noodles at *pho* stalls and feeling like you know the place well, though you may never have ventured near the endless rows of new apartment blocks that pimple the outskirts.

Now there's money to be made, the conflicts of the last century have been confined to the museums, so don't come here looking for your Graham Greene moment, even if you do check into his room (number 228 since you ask) at the <u>Sofitel Metropole</u> hotel (see p018), or expecting the charming but tenacious people of Hanoi to conform to Hollywood type.

ESSENTIAL INFO
FACTS, FIGURES AND USEFUL ADDRESSES

TOURIST OFFICE
Vietnam Tourism
30a Pho Ly Thuong Kiet
T 826 4089
www.vn-tourism.com

TRANSPORT
Car hire
Exotissimo Travel
61 Ly Thai To
T 935 1400
Sinhcafe Travel
30 Hang Be
T 836 5353
Taxis
Hanoi Taxi
T 853 5353
Van Xuan Taxi
T 822 2888

EMERGENCY SERVICES
Ambulance
T 115
Fire
T 114
Police
T 113
24-hour pharmacy
Family Medical Practice
298 Pho Kim Ma
T 843 0748
www.vietnammedicalpractice.com

EMBASSIES
British Embassy
31 Pho Hai Ba Trung
T 936 0500
www.britishembassy.gov.uk/vietnam
United States Embassy
7 Lang Ha
T 850 5000
hanoi.usembassy.gov

MONEY
American Express
Exotissimo Travel
26 Tran Nhat Duat
T 828 2150
travel.americanexpress.com

POSTAL SERVICES
Post Office
6 Dinh Le
T 825 7036
Shipping
UPS
77 Lang Ha
T 514 288
www.ups.com

BOOKS
A Bright Shining Lie by Neil Sheehan (Picador)
Hanoi: Biography of a City by William Stewart Logan (University of New South Wales Press)
The Sorrow of War by Bao Ninh (Vintage)

WEBSITE
Newspaper
vietnamnews.vnanet.vn

COST OF LIVING
Taxi from Noi Bai International Airport to city centre
£7.50
Cappuccino
£1.25
Packet of cigarettes
£0.75
Daily newspaper
£0.35
Bottle of champagne
£12.50

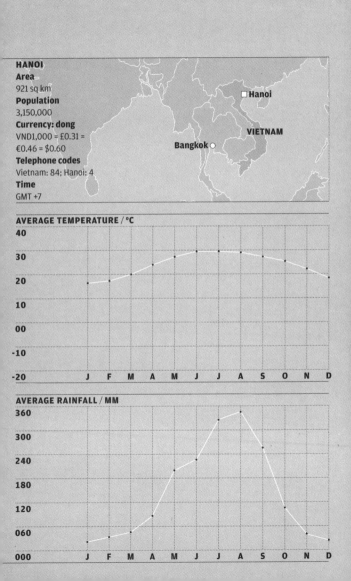

HANOI

Area
921 sq km

Population
3,150,000

Currency: dong
VND1,000 = £0.31 =
€0.46 = $0.60

Telephone codes
Vietnam: 84; Hanoi: 4

Time
GMT +7

AVERAGE TEMPERATURE / °C

AVERAGE RAINFALL / MM

NEIGHBOURHOODS
THE AREAS YOU NEED TO KNOW AND WHY

To help you navigate the city, we've chosen the most interesting districts (see below and the map inside the back cover) and colour-coded our featured venues, according to their location; those venues that are outside these areas are not coloured.

TAY HO

The vast West Lake lies at the centre of this increasingly suburban zone, which has drawn many locals away from Hoan Kiem, thanks to its rapidly expanding housing and peaceful atmosphere. The lake itself is actually shrinking, due to the frenetic development along its edge.

BA DINH

French colonial villas, now mostly occupied by embassies, and overbearing brutalist buildings dedicated to Ho Chi Minh, such as the Mausoleum (see p010) and Museum (see p027), are peppered throughout this leafy government zone. It was in Ba Dinh Square, on 2 September 1945, that Ho declared Vietnam an independent state.

THANH XUAN

Visit this outlying district on a Saturday to watch a show at the Water Puppet Theatre (361 Doung Truong Chinh, T 853 4545). And if you're planning on leaving town, you can catch a helicopter from Bach Mai domestic airport to Ha Long Bay (see p097).

HOAN KIEM

The artisanal Old Quarter, located on the north side of Hoan Kiem Lake (see p025), represents the heart of Hanoi. Its '36 Streets', a dense and bustling network of lanes, is still the domain of the city's craftsmen. In the early morning, the park around the lake is the place to go jogging or watch Hanoians practise tai chi.

HAI BA TRUNG

This area boasts one of Hanoi's most popular green zones, Lenin Park. Once the city's rubbish tip, it was transformed by Ho Chi Minh, who added gardens, paths and statues. East of the park is the Lien Phai Pagoda (42 Ngo Chua Lien Phai), which is tiered like a wedding cake.

CAU GIAY

Amid the non-descript high rises and office blocks lies the T-shaped Ha Pagoda, secret meeting place for the Communist Party of Vietnam during the First Indochina War. Also in the area are the Vietnam Museum of Ethnology (Nguyen Van Huyen) and My Way Seafood Restaurant (17T3 Hoang Dao Thuy), famous for its spring rolls.

DONG DA

The Confucian Temple of Literature (see p014), Vietnam's most important temple complex, is the main draw of this mostly residential neighbourhood. If you take the train, you'll pass through the International Style Hanoi Railway Station (see p062).

TU LIEM

Around 12km north-west of central Hanoi, Tu Liem is filling up fast with apartment towers and office blocks. Football fans flock here to the 40,000-seat My Dinh National Stadium (see p092), while world leaders convene at the impressive Hanoi National Convention Center (see p057) by Germany's Von Gerkan, Marg and Partners.

LANDMARKS

THE SHAPE OF THE CITY SKYLINE

Not as brashly thrusting as young Ho Chi Minh City, Hanoi took its time throwing up office towers and anonymous apartment blocks, but it is catching up fast, and the built environment, especially on the outskirts, is changing at a frenetic pace. The city even has that most un-Asian and un-communist of things, a heritage movement that wants to slow the pace of change.

Nevertheless, in the centre of the city there is not much room for development and, consequently, not much opportunity for a skyscraper-filled skyline. Instead, central Hanoi maintains an intimate, human scale, which is one of the things that makes it so fabulously appealing, whether in the tight lanes of the Old Quarter or the tree-lined boulevards created by the French. The Hanoi Towers complex (see po68), built on the site of an old prison ironically dubbed the 'Hanoi Hilton' by American POWs, is about as lofty as it gets, but even if the towers do occasionally prove a visual cue to help you get your bearings, they are architecturally undistinguished. You need to look to the past for many of the city's most pleasing prominent features, whether they be from the Ly dynasty, in the form of the Temple of Literature (see po14), the French colonial period, such as the Hanoi Opera House (po13), or the era of Soviet technical assistance, with its concrete-centric monuments, such as the Ho Chi Minh Mausoleum (see po10).
For full addresses, see Resources.

Ho Chi Minh Mausoleum
Hanoi can thank various treaties with
the Soviet Union for the appearance of
monumental brutalism in its midst in the
mid-1970s. The Soviet influence can be
seen most clearly at Uncle Ho's final resting
place, a granite and concrete colonnaded
box put up under the supervision of Garold
Grigorevich Isakovich. Be respectful in
what you wear and check it's open first.
1 Bach Thao, T 234 4760

Lenin statue

There are not many places left, outside of North Korea and Budapest's Statue Park, where you can still see a good-sized statue of the original bald Bolshevik. Hanoi's is another gift from the period when Comrade Isakovich was leaving his mark on the city. Lenin's birthday, on 22 April, sees delegations of deputy general secretaries and people's council members lining up to lay wreaths at the old boy's feet, but it's force of habit rather than a sustained ideological commitment. In 2006, on that same day in April, the National Assembly meeting was halted so that party leaders could have their photo taken with Bill Gates.

Dien Bien Phu

Hanoi Opera House

The model for Hanoi's Opera House was the Opéra Garnier in Paris, but while the original has been called an 'overloaded sideboard', its neo-baroque tropical imitation has lost just enough of the superfluous squiggles to be quietly pleasing. Opened in 1911 as the physical manifestation of the colonists' 'civilising mission', it looks like the kind of place you go to start a revolution, which is just what the Viet Minh did in 1945. It hosted socialist realist performances for decades, but gradually fell into disrepair. Following a three-year renovation under the direction of Vietnamese architects Ho Thieu Tri and Hoang Phuc Sinh, the Opera House opened again in 1997, its miles of marble gleaming, the gilt all aglitter. You have to buy a ticket for a performance to have a look inside.
1 Trang Tien, T 933 0113

Temple of Literature
Despite being restored to within
an inch of its life, this 900-year-old
Confucian Temple of Literature is the
best idea you're going to get of how the
royal quarter once looked. Part of a
plan of five walled courtyards, the main
buildings, all swooping red-tiled roofs,
carved wood and sharp brickwork, are
a peaceful place to amble about.
Pho Van Mieu, T 942 1061

HOTELS

WHERE TO STAY AND WHICH ROOMS TO BOOK

For a long time after the Vietnam war, Hanoi's hotel sector pretty much comprised crumbling colonial-era greats and travellers' digs. International groups and foreign money started to invest in hotel property during the 1990s, only for this to come to a shuddering halt with the 1997 Asian Tiger meltdown – in the case of Hanoi, this meant the Sheraton Hotel (see p020) stood unfinished for seven years. Things picked up again after the start of the new millennium, and now Hanoi has a collection of business-traveller behemoths, including the Daewoo Hotel (360 Pho Kim Ma, T 831 5000) and the Sofitel Plaza (1 Duong Thanh Nien, T 823 8888), while the Sofitel Metropole (overleaf) has been revamped several times and the Hilton Hanoi Opera (see p022) now denotes a pleasure palace rather than a place of torture. And more are on the way: the InterContinental and Novotel chains both have developments in the pipeline.

Interestingly, a generation of shiny new hotels are joining the semi-luxury market from the other end. In several cases, so-so and budget options in the Old and French Quarters have been spruced up with the designer boutique market in mind. So far, the only examples truly worthy of a recommendation are the Zéphyr (4 and 6 Pho Ba Trieu, T 934 1256) and the Church Hotel (opposite), both of which fill up fast in the peak autumn season. *For full addresses and room rates, see Resources.*

Church Hotel

The Church has been given an upgrade that almost takes it to designer boutique standards. The Superior Doubles (above), which are decorated in a simple, modern fashion – white with dark furniture and floors – are the rooms to choose. There's not much space, but then you are in the jam-packed Old Quarter. Best of all, the hotel sits between fashion boutiques and cafés in the area's most happening street, the tree-lined Nha Tho. You are at the heart of the action, so you have to make allowances for noise, but for what it is, this hotel is very good value, although you do hear the occasional complaint about the hauteur of some of the staff. The Church's sister hotel, Thien Tan (T 824 4005), on Cha Ca, sometimes acts as an overspill. *9 Nha Tho, T 928 8118, www.churchhotel.com.vn*

Sofitel Metropole
They make much of the Graham Greene connection here, but the whole building is a repository of Hanoi history: coups, invasions, peace treaties, Jane Fonda's protesting era. The Metropole's location is unbeatable, and so is the service. Soak up the atmosphere in a room, such as the Opera Suite (pictured), in the old wing.
15 Ngo Quyen, T 826 6919,
www.sofitel.com

Sheraton Hotel

Located just 10 minutes by taxi from the Old Quarter, the Sheraton provides the high (and highly standardised) quality you would expect to find in a five-star: the rooms are neat, the bathrooms are big, the lobby (above) is opulent and the service is unobtrusively good. Perched on a spur of land sticking into the West Lake, it provides superb views, especially from the Executive Suites on the 18th floor. The neighbourhood is something of an expat barrio, and the excellent in-house Hemispheres restaurant (see p046) attracts plenty of non-resident trade.
K5 Nghi Tam, 11 Xuan Dieu, T 719 9000, www.starwoodhotels.com

Gia Bao Hotel

Opened in 2006, this little gem of a hotel is about as close as Hanoi gets to proper boutique accommodation in the heart of the Old Quarter, but choose your room wisely. Of the 28 available, some of the cheaper ones don't have much light, so opt for one of the nine suites, or the best room of all, VIP 701 (above), which has a charming roof terrace with great views over Hoan Kiem Lake (see p025). Beware the other 'VIP' room, 101 (the irony): its light comes from a balcony overlooking the lobby. Room 504 is spacious and looks out over the neighbourhood. Suite 401 is smaller but boasts a little private balcony. Good-value tariffs, along with an excellent location and friendly, helpful staff, further ensure the appeal of this place.
38 Lo Su, T 935 1494,
www.giabaohanoihotel.com

Hilton Hanoi Opera

Perhaps not surprisingly, the Hilton chain decided to append the word Opera to its Hanoi hotel name – plus it's slam next door to the French colonial Opera House (see p013). The curving, pale yellow Hilton was built to match its neighbour, and on the inside sticks with the idea of grand dramatic displays. Think marble, distant ceilings and a massive chandelier by Philippe Pascal of Art'Ur. And that's just the lobby (above). The rooms are not so baroque, decorated with simple paintings, embroideries and traditional furniture. The best are the five on the fifth floor, their balconies overlooking the Opera House.
1 Pho Le Thanh Tong, T 933 0500,
www.hanoi.hilton.com

Meliá

The Meliá is what it is: a briskly efficient, if somewhat stodgy, enormous executives' hotel. It does a lot of business by catering for large conference groups, and it's a big hit with the show-off wedding market. So far, so typical of the Asian luxury hotel sector. But the rooms are sumptuous and large and the city views are superb, particularly from the Executive Suites (above). Service is impressively personal for such an anonymous behemoth, and the amenities are all there when and where you want them. Better still, the growth in competition in the city means there are deals to be had, particularly online.
44b Pho Ly Thuong Kiet, T 934 3343, www.meliahanoi.com

24 HOURS

SEE THE BEST OF THE CITY IN JUST ONE DAY

The typical Hanoian day is one that starts early and finishes relatively early, for it is not a late-night party city. But it is a noisy, frantic place right from the get-go, which is usually around 5am. Thankfully, you're a visitor and you can indulge in a lie-in – we have started your schedule sometime after 6am, when you do your workout. After that, we've chosen a cool, modern breakfast spot, Les Comptoirs (see p026), followed by a wander around the Ho Chi Minh Museum (see p027) – a cultural experience that is anything but cool or modern, and all the better for it.

Mid-afternoon, we throw you into the Old Quarter where, if anything, the city's pace seems even more high pressured because it is trapped in the narrow streets. But take it easy, you can always step back from the manic mopeds or the fish hawkers to enjoy a pleasant trundle up and down its atmospheric byways. Yes, you will probably be in someone's way, but, hey, isn't that just what tourists do to you in your home city? While in this neighbourhood, head for Hang Ma, street of the paper goods, and buy a votive paper television to send to an ancestor in the afterlife. It could work. And for when the noise and the dust and the heat and incessant traffic get too much, we've picked out an oasis of calm, Green Tangerine (see p030), where you can rest up and sample some great cuisine to end your perfect Hanoi day.

For full addresses, see Resources.

06.00-08.00 Hoan Kiem Lake

Do as the locals do and get some early-morning exercise. Head for Hoan Kiem Lake to join the joggers, speed-walkers and tai chi practitioners burning up, or just waving their limbs around slowly, on the strip of parkland that surrounds the water. It may not be the biggest lake in the world – in fact, you can walk around it in half an hour – but for Hanoians, Hoan Kiem and the red lacquered Huc Bridge

(above) are the heart of their city, a kind of aquatic Trafalgar Square. The name translates as 'Lake of the Restored Sword' and commemorates the rather Arthurian legend of King Le Thai To, who vanquished the Chinese with the help of a magical sword he fished from the lake. A turtle, rather than a waterlogged lady, claimed the weapon back for the gods when the fighting was done.

08.30 Les Comptoirs
A neat, wood-panelled café in the lobby of the Press Club (see p034) building, Les Comptoirs is something of a haven from the bustle and noise that will attack you for the rest of the day. It serves a high-quality range of local and imported teas and coffees plus excellent fresh pastries. You can pick up an international paper or magazine here, the building has a free wi-fi connection and it's a good choice for a casual but quiet breakfast meeting. The clientele is a mixture of hacks, the odd tourist, expats and local business types. Les Comptoirs also sells books, fine teas, coffees, local crafts and photography.
59a Ly Thai To, T 934 0888,
www.hanoi-pressclub.com

10.30 Ho Chi Minh Museum

Another brutalist blast from the Russian architect Garold Gregorievich Isakovitch, who designed the Ho Chi Minh Mausoleum (see p010), this angular white wedge of a building opened in 1990 to commemorate the 100th anniversary of Ho's birth. Despite the swathes of concrete, the museum is supposed to represent a lotus flower, the Buddhist symbol for perfect understanding: Ho Chi Minh means 'he who enlightens'.

You don't need a forensic knowledge of the 1940s Vietnamese Communist Party to enjoy this museum, just a willingness to indulge the curator's odd metaphorical interpretations of concepts like 'peace', 'the future' and 'youth'. The building has a crazy Soviet beauty all of its own and is worth a hike around. They literally don't make them like this any more.
3 Pho Ngoc Ha

14.00 Hoan Kiem

Although the walls are long gone and
only one gate remains, Hanoi's thriving
Old Quarter is a fascinating part of
the city worth exploring. Key features
include the ludicrously narrow, ancient
'tube houses', which were designed to
circumvent land-tax rules. Look out for
the artisans' streets with 500-year-old
names – 'Hang', meaning merchandise,
appears in many of them.

20.00 Green Tangerine

French chef Benjamin Rascalou whips up modern French cuisine with an innovative Vietnamese twist at this lovely restaurant in Hoan Kiem. It's housed in a carefully restored 1928 colonial villa, reached via a courtyard. Since Rascalou and his Franco-Vietnamese partner, Stefan Yvin, opened it in July 2003, the restaurant has been a firm fixture among Hanoi's foodies and its ever-growing community of expats. Signature dishes include a better-than-it-sounds rack of lamb served in coffee and a splendid lasagne stuffed with a pâté of crab and broccoli cooked in cognac. For dessert, try the fried banana crispy spring rolls with coconut ice cream and chilli. Although the high-ceilinged rooms inside the villa are elegant and pleasantly airy, the real treat is the tile-lined garden with its tangerine trees. Book well in advance.
48 Hang Be, T 825 1286

URBAN LIFE

CAFÉS, RESTAURANTS, BARS AND NIGHTCLUBS

Vietnam has one of the great culinary cultures in the world. It has been influenced by Chinese invaders, Thai neighbours, Indian traders and, of course, French imperialists, but it also has its own distinctive elements, which are ideally suited to modern palates used to light, fresh foods with complex flavour combinations. Put more simply, it involves lots of salty, sweet and chilli ingredients. In the south of the country, regional food snobs have tended to dismiss Hanoi cooking as the same as their own, only made bland, but if that were ever true, it certainly isn't now. With options from the humble street *pho* stall to a growing number of designer restaurants housed in colonial villas, your main dining dilemma is what to choose when so much is so good.

Nightlife is a different matter. Whether it's owing to the usual government-town conservatism or something more deeply rooted, there just aren't that many Hanoians who want to stay up late. Smaller restaurants expect to be sweeping up by 9pm, and even at weekends it can be a struggle to find somewhere selling alcohol after midnight, not least because the government tries to enforce a curfew. Yet the lounging, bar-club scene is burgeoning and is already much improved on a few years ago. Its small scale also means you need never feel you're missing out on a better party elsewhere – all the beautiful people will probably be with you. *For full addresses, see Resources.*

Wild Lotus

The most recent restaurant from the owners of established upscale eateries Wild Rice (T 943 8896) and Moon River (T 871 1658), Wild Lotus wouldn't look out of place in Venice Beach or Hoxton. The décor is softly contemporary, with elegantly repeated lotus patterns, and great use is made of the high-ceilinged space on the second floor. The food is well-executed contemporary Asian fusion, with Western touches. Corn and leek soup with crab and coriander dumplings has been a big hit, but the menu is regularly updated with twists on regional specialities – mains include a fish tikka in pandanus leaves.
52 Nguyen Du, T 943 9342

Press Club
Opened in 1997 by the Vietnamese
Journalists Association, the Press Club
is housed in a colonial villa converted by
architect Brigitte Dumont de Chassart.
It features The Deli bistro, Les Comptoirs
café (see p026) and a large restaurant
terrace that is Hanoi high society's
venue of choice for general good times.
*59a Ly Thai To, T 934 0888,
www.hanoi-pressclub.com*

Le Beaulieu

The fine dining restaurant at the Sofitel Metropole (see p018) has been serving up Hanoi's most revered classical French cuisine for more than 100 years and remains a place for both tourists and the city's well-to-do to see and be seen. Although victim to numerous renovations, it preserves some colonial splendour, but now with a hint of contemporary French architecture. The marble and wood is still there in abundance, but chandeliers and large windows brighten things up. The service is as you'd expect in Paris, that is to say relatively sullen, and some whisper that the menu hasn't kept up with the improved quality elsewhere in the city, but the seafood buffet is divine. This remains a destination restaurant.
Sofitel Metropole, 15 Ngo Quyen, T 826 6919, www.sofitel.com

Ly Club

Housed in a splendid art deco pile that was formerly the residence of the Chief Banker, the Ly Club opened in 2004 and is named after the imperial dynasty that kicked out the Chinese – the owner is a descendant. The villa is authentically club-like, with its collection of Ly dynasty antiques, huge heavy-scented flowers and potted plants, and very deep armchairs. The refined air is added to by the pianist (although some nights you may suffer a guitarist playing covers of Western torch songs), handmade china and sumptuous service. The food is not bad, either, with separate Vietnamese and Western menus. The fried scallops with diced apple come highly recommended, as does a refreshing drink at the bar – the Bombay Sapphire martini is a winner.
51 Ly Thai To, T 936 3069,
www.club51lythaito.vn

Bamboo Bar

You can try to kid yourself that you're a cynical and drink-sodden Graham Greene character by sitting under a ceiling fan in the courtyard bar at the Metropole (see p018), but the proximity of the modern swimming pool and numerous wealthy tourists will probably blow your literary fantasy. Nevertheless, the simple, white, wooden-roofed Bamboo Bar remains a good choice for a late-evening digestif and cigar. The service is impeccable and the surroundings lushly luxurious. It is calm and quiet, an escape within the city, except at weekends when it is a popular destination for Hanoi's newest generation of thrusting, successful business types.
Sofitel Metropole, 15 Ngo Quyen, T 826 6919, www.sofitel.com

I-Box

Think eclectic furniture, faux leopardskin, lots of velvet and hand-painted wallpaper, and pretty, parading cigarette girls, and you get a fair idea of what to expect at bar/restaurant/lounging spot I-Box. It's a look that could have been picked up wholesale from the Marais, and it has proved a hit with Hanoi's rich kids. In fact, it's the sister to a Ho Chi Minh City bar of the same name that has been attracting the burgeoning bourgeoisie for a decade. I-Box's wine selection is impressive and the baby back pork ribs get good reviews, but drinks and the food are not really the point here. Rather more importantly, the venue provides a splendid backdrop against which to pose and preen. Let's just say that the fake open fire isn't the only thing in the room that thinks it's hot. *32 Le Thai To, T 828 8820*

Café Pho Co

A hidden gem with many local adherents, Café Pho Co is found only after you pass through the My Nghes art and souvenir shop on busy Hang Gai. You leave all the noise and bustle of the Old Quarter behind you once you get through the shop and into a tiny alley, where you'll see an old villa wreathed in foliage and birdsong. Follow the steps up to reach the café on the roof and a fabulous view of the Hoan Kiem Lake. There is also a temple in the building, so expect to spot the odd priest. Although there is probably better coffee to be found and the snacks here are nothing to write home about, as a peaceful place to while away a few hours, there's nowhere quite like this in Hanoi.
11 Pho Hang Bai, T 828 5080

Vine Wine Boutique Bar & Café
Located in the expat enclave of Tay Ho, Vine is run by Montreal-born Donald Berger. He has worked in Hong Kong, Bangkok, Monte Carlo, London and Paris (with Alain Ducasse) and is married to a Vietnamese textile artist whose work makes appearances on the walls and furnishings at Vine. The comprehensive menu is contemporary international, spanning antipasti, sashimi and a porcini mushroom soup with truffles. The signature entrée is flame-grilled blue fin tuna steak with horseradish and potato purée with truffle oil. The wine list runs to 1,200 labels, mainly from the New World, and Vine also carries a range of some of the better quality *ruou can* rice liquors, as well as a couple of tipples with dead snakes in the bottle.
3 Xuan Dieu, T 719 8000,
www.vine-group.com

Solace
Housed in a boat on the Red River,
Solace inherited its hipster crowd from
Hanoi's original late-night lounge boat,
Titanic, which, appropriately enough,
sank in 2006. At weekends, DJ Tuan
Anh plays Vietnamese housey-tranceish
tunes. During the week, a more mellow
mood prevails, with sets from live bands.
End of Chuong Duong, T 935 0960,
www.solacebar.com

Hemispheres

The dining experience at the Sheraton (see p020) is partly about the food and partly about the location of your table. If the weather is good, reserve a spot on the terrace overlooking the West Lake, and suck up a view that is considerably more pleasing than watching chef Sven Neuert and his Vietnamese sous, Nguyen Hu Phuoc Set, clatter their pans in the open kitchen. Nevertheless, what that clattering produces is as fine a selection of modern Vietnamese cuisine and Asian-fusion flavours as you will find in the city. Think crab ragout garnished with local herbs, or southern Vietnamese blue crab in tamarind sauce. Finish with blossom tea, and watch as the flower head in the glass opens its petals.

Sheraton Hotel, K5 Nghi Tam, 11 Xuan Dieu, T 719 9000, www.starwoodhotels.com

Emperor

Offering some of the best cuisine and arguably the best setting of all Hanoi restaurants, the Emperor is something of a legend. Book several days ahead for dinner and try to specify a table on the balcony of the traditional stilt house or on the patio of the newer villa. The menu is dominated by Hue dishes, such as fish wrapped in banana leaves, and by sweet and spicy numbers from the south, such as beef with honey, or tiger prawns with tamarind. It is reputedly Hanoi's most expensive restaurant, but still expect to pay about a quarter what you would in London. The setting is decidedly romantic. If you want something less intimate, there is a jazz bar downstairs with live music.
18b Pho Le Thanh Tong, T 826 8801

XY Café & Bar

Since opening in 2006, XY Café & Bar has quickly been adopted by Hanoi's hip young things, ever on the lookout for somewhere new that closes late (1am) and isn't a dive. Downstairs, the neon lighting is a bit harsh, but upstairs there is a terrace and chairs slung so low you may be able to see the flat-screen TVs mounted perversely in the ceiling.
7 Ly Dao Thanh, T 936 6156

Ba Mien

Thanks to Brigitte Dumont de Chassart, who designed the Press Club (see p034), the contemporary styling of the Ba Mien restaurant at the Hilton Hanoi Opera (see p022) is strikingly better than that of most Asian chain-hotel eateries. Thanks to its good looks, Ba Mien has become a favourite destination of expats and local scenesters since it opened in the summer of 2006. Oversized steel chairs are a fairly wacky design statement for Hanoi, and the terrace, with its sleek glass roof, is a pleasant place to lounge over a late-night cocktail. The menu brings together Vietnam's three food regions: the crisp, healthy taste of the north, imperial delicacies from Hue, and the hotter flavours of the south. The poached lobster on the menu at Ba Mien is famously served screamingly fresh.

Hilton Hanoi Opera, 1 Pho Le Thanh Tong, T 933 0500, www.hilton.com

Bobby Chinn
Born in New Zealand, British-educated and of Chinese and Egyptian descent, Bobby Chinn is a big mover in the Vietnamese restaurant scene. At his Hanoi restaurant, the silk-partitioned nooks and crannies of the back dining room (pictured) are the place to be seen, while the bar at the front attracts a good-looking cocktail crowd.
1 Pho Ba Trieu, T 934 8577,
www.bobbychinn.com

INSIDER'S GUIDE

HA LINH THU, FASHION DESIGNER

From a graphic design background, Linh Thu worked on local newspaper *Lao Dong* before starting her own business. Although she has no formal training, she is now the leading fashion designer in Hanoi, and has two Hoan Kiem boutiques dedicated to her label Pearl Ha (www.pearlha.com), one located at the Hilton Hanoi Opera (see p022) and the other at 40 Hang Bong (T 825 7650). Linh Thu finds that she doesn't need to venture far from her base in the centre of the city. She likes to start her day early at Nuôi Café (Luong Van Can). If time allows, she will pop into Thang Long Bookshop (53-55 Pho Trang Tien, T 825 7043) to stock up on the latest publications, before heading to her favourite eaterie, Baan Thai (3b Cha Ca, T 828 8588), for a delicious lunch.

In the evenings, Linh Thu likes to watch movies with friends at the Megastar Cineplex in Vincom City Tower (191 Pho Ba Trieu, T 974 3333). If she wants Vietnamese food for dinner, she heads to Sen Restaurant (Lane 431, 10 Au Co, T 719 9242). Linh Thu is also a regular at the Japanese eaterie Totoya (322 Pho Ba Trieu, T 821 6033). For a relaxed after-work drink, she likes to drop in to the Golden Cock (5 Bao Khanh). And when she's in the mood to party or wants to celebrate a new collection, Linh Thu's chosen venue is Solace (see p044), or the sinking Titanic, as locals like to call it, where she can listen to live music or hit the dancefloor. *For full addresses, see Resources.*

ARCHITOUR
A GUIDE TO HANOI'S ICONIC BUILDINGS

The grand avenues of Hanoi were designed to attract colonisers and show the locals how superior French civilisation was when compared with their own. This they did, given that most of the vermilion palaces of the old dynasty had been flattened in the late 19th century by the civilised French. After WWII, the Vietnamese were pretty much occupied with expelling occupiers and were suffering under state planning and an American embargo, so they didn't put up many major buildings, apart from the occasional Soviet-inspired museum. Economic liberalisation and growth have brought some new hotels, offices and clusters of faceless apartment blocks on the periphery, but nothing to compete with the elegant neo-baroque and deco structures of the Union of Indochina. Most of these were overseen by Auguste Henri Vildieu, the city's chief architect at the turn of the 20th century. Luckily for us, and for Hanoi's best restaurateurs, Nixon's notorious Christmas 1972 bombing of the city left most of Vildieu's work untouched.

New money has seen the colonial buildings being spruced up to attract the tourist dollar. What was built from exploitation is now in turn being exploited. If all the history gets too much, you can always travel a few miles out of the centre, to the new Hanoi National Convention Center (opposite), to see some high-quality contemporary architecture and get a taste of Vietnam's future. *For full addresses, see Resources.*

Hanoi National Convention Center

Germany's Von Gerkan, Marg and Partners knocked up the National Convention Center in just 26 months, so it would be ready for the 2006 Asia-Pacific Economic Summit. It was meant to impress on the 26 visiting world leaders, including Bush and Putin, how modern and go-getting Vietnam has become. The building pretty much does the job. Its diminishing wave roof, with a kind of ship's bridge emerging from it, is jauntily nautical. Inside, the various lobby areas are all lofty white reinforced concrete (overleaf) and the auditorium is jaw-dropping in scale and golden-hued in finish. But then it should be – it cost £150m to build. Take a taxi out to My Dinh to witness just how important architecture is for developing countries with one shot at the international limelight.

My Dinh, Me Tri

Long Bien Bridge

The steel latticework of this cantilevered bridge, designed by Monsieur Eiffel and opened in 1902, has a little of the look of his tower, only lying on its side. The 1.6km structure was known as Paul Doumer Bridge until Vietnamese independence in 1945, Doumer being the governor who oversaw infrastructure development of the Union of Indochina at the start of the 20th century. The bridge connects Hanoi by rail to the port of Haiphong and to China's Yunnan province, hence its attraction during the war to American bombers. The Vietnamese always repaired it quickly, and the bridge became a symbol of national resistance. It is no longer safe for road traffic, but pedestrians, cyclists and trains can enjoy a pleasant crossing.

Turtle Tower

The Golden Turtle, Kim Qui, who is said to live in Hoan Kiem Lake, is closely associated with the history of Hanoi, and makes auspicious appearances on national anniversaries. It stars in the story of the restored sword, after which Hoan Kiem Lake is named, and many assume, local and visitor alike, that this tower was put up by King Le Loi in the 15th century to commemorate the legend of the sword, after his victory over the Ming dynasty. In fact, it was built in 1886, by a mandarin, as a resting place for his father. The two-storey stupa has become a symbol of the city to compete with the wooden One Pillar Pagoda, built in 1049 and one of the few surviving structures from the original city, and efforts to restore it have met with local resistance.

Hoan Kiem Lake

Hanoi Railway Station
After North Vietnamese independence
in 1954, students travelled to the Soviet
Union and Warsaw Pact countries to be
trained in various technical disciplines.
As you can see here, the architects were
schooled in the International Style. This
concrete building, completed in 1972,
stands as one of the first signs of
Russian influence on the city.
120 Duong Le Duan, T 942 3697

Hanoi Flag Tower

Known locally as Cot Co, the Flag Tower is one of the few architectural works in Hanoi that was not destroyed by the French in the 1890s. Instead, it was used by French troops as an observation tower and communication station. It stands in the grounds of the fascinating Military History Museum (T 823 4264) in the citadel. This is the place to which you head to see an American tank, bits of shot-down US warplane and some great archive footage of the wars against the French and the Americans. The exhibition leaves you with little doubt that the Vietnamese were always going to win independence. You can climb to the terrace below the tower for a view across the army headquarters. *Dien Bien Phu*

Central Post Office

Hanoi's main post office offers a telling contrast with the French colonial one in Ho Chi Minh City. The latter, designed by Gustave Eiffel, resembles an elegant European train station – all wrought ironwork and glazing. Hanoi's austere, concrete number looks like it should have helicopters on its flat roof, helping the last of the Americans flee the country. Yet this tropical dictator-tecture, on the banks of Hoan Kiem Lake, has a classical-modernist charm of its own. It was from here in the 1970s that loudspeakers used to blare out the patriotic pop tune, *In Praise of Ho Chi Minh*, every morning at 6am to rouse the workers. Now, it's a place where wireless broadband is authorised and 3G networks flogged to foreign investors.
Dinh Tien Hoang

Hanoi Towers

This hotel and luxury apartment complex is a symbol not just of the *doi moi* (renewal) reform policies the government instituted in the 1980s, but of how Vietnam is dealing with its past and future. It was built on the grounds of the old Hoa Lo prison, known to American airmen, including John McCain, as the 'Hanoi Hilton'. In fact, thousands more Vietnamese died there, under the French, than Americans ever did. Many argued that the whole place should be swept away, consigning a dark memory to the past. But veterans, both Vietnamese and American, lobbied for the prison to be kept as an historic monument. In the end, the government built the towers on the site of 80 per cent of the prison and created a museum memorial. Legend has it that a specialist had to reconfigure the building to appease an army of ghosts that were stopping locals from taking up residence.
49 Pho Hai Ba Trung

State Bank

Standing at the head of a plaza that leads down to Hoan Kiem Lake, the State Bank was pretty much the first word in Vietnamese modernism when it was built by architect Georges André Trouvé in 1930. It displays art deco touches with Asian ornamentation, but its best feature is the ribbed dome, which has a weird, flying-saucerish air.
49 Ly Thai To, T 825 4818

SHOPPING

THE BEST RETAIL THERAPY AND WHAT TO BUY

Hanoi's shopping scene is concentrated mainly in the Old Quarter, in the network of busy little streets around St Joseph Cathedral, notably Nha Tho, Pho Nha Chung, Hang Gai and Hang Trong. Here you'll find endless displays of good-quality, low-cost ceramics, silk (rarely 100 per cent pure), embroidery, stone carvings, lacquerware and art, as befits Hanoi and northern Vietnam's reputation as the more cultured end of the country. But that's not to say there aren't thrusting entrepreneurs here in abundance. Among the fashion boutiques, everyone is looking to export and everyone wants an international reputation. Products that have already made it include the colourful beaded handbags of Tina Sparkle (17 Nha Tho, T 928 7616), which is the little sister boutique of Hanoi's most successful fashion label, Ipa-Nima (see p076). Other independent stores, such as Le Vent (see p080), are doing good business by combining traditional styling with contemporary design.

Hang Gai is the street to head for if you're looking for tailors who can make anything to order, from a traditional silk tunic to a man's three-piece suit, in a matter of days and at a fraction of Western prices (a good option as Vietnamese sizes tend to be snug on Occidental frames). And finally, stroll down Hang Bong to find the Vietnamese Communist Party posters, banners and badges that (sort of) helped to defeat a superpower.

For full addresses, see Resources.

Foot badminton

At its best, foot badminton, or *da cau*, is a sport for the urban slacker who doesn't like to put too much effort in; you don't have to change into any fancy sportswear, you don't need to play on a special pitch, and the equipment is nothing more than a feathered shuttlecock. Men stand around in circles, jackets over their arms, talking on their phones while kicking the shuttle to each other. It's like hacky sack without the annoying American teens. At its most energetic, you use a net and play like a dervish in the national championships. The game originated in China, where it was part of military training in the 11th century, but Vietnam has made it its national sport. Pick up the shuttles and nets at street stands in the Old Quarter.

Art Vietnam Gallery
Located in a stunning four-storey 'tube house', Art Vietnam is the city's most interesting contemporary gallery. Its director, Suzanne Lecht, has been at the forefront of the Hanoi scene since 1994. She holds monthly exhibitions, studio tours and educational workshops, and encourages new and experimental work.
30 Hang Than, T 927 2349, www.artvietnamgallery.com

Ipa-Nima

Christina Yu was a Hong Kong litigator with a fetish for handbags and shoes. When her husband took a job in Hanoi, she came with him, gave up the bar and started this handbag business. The designs are hers and the hand-embroidered craftsmanship is Vietnam's. After producing bags for GOD, Shanghai Tang and Anteprima, she developed her own collection and now exports to Barney's NY, Harvey Nichols in London, Ginza in Tokyo and The Swank Shop in Hong Kong. Her shop has attracted visiting dignitaries, such as Hillary Clinton, but Yu's bags are rather more quirky than that makes them sound. She even does a sequined tote with Mao or Che's face on it, which lets you know all you need about the state of Vietnamese socialism.

34 Han Thuyen, T 933 4000,
www.ipa-nima.com

Marena Hanoi

The Vietnamese have worked with lacquer for more than 2,000 years and you won't go far in the Old Quarter without seeing lacquerware piled high in store windows. The difficulty lies in finding the real deal: lacquerware made the traditional way, with the resin of the *Rhus succedanea* tree, rather than imported Japanese lacquer and artificial chemicals. Two shops worth seeking out are the family-run Minh Tam (2 Hang Bong), which specialises in huge plates, vases and masks, often featuring eggshells under as many as 20 layers of lacquer, and the larger Marena Hanoi, which combines contemporary Japanese design standards with traditional Vietnamese production methods. Marena exports to Japan, America and Australia, but is also willing to take a customer's design and produce something bespoke in a matter of days.

28 Pho Nha Chung, T 828 5542

Le Vent

This blink-and-you'll-miss it boutique belongs to one of the most interesting young fashion designers now working in Hanoi. Former corporate lawyer Lee Huyen has been designing simple but highly alluring feminine couture since 2002. Her pieces incorporate traditional Vietnamese lines and sleek, contemporary cuts. Some of her dresses are unforgivingly tight, as befits the land of the *ao dai*, but everything is extremely well finished. In addition to dresses, she sells silk blouses, scarves, shawls, organza curtains and wall hangings. Huyen's range tends to come in small sizes, so if you happen to be larger than the average Vietnamese fashionista, you can have an item made to measure.
103 Hang Gai

Paper doll

Vietnamese paper crafts have numerous incarnations. Ancestor worship may see the burning of many a miniature dollar bill, motorbike, car or house, while delicately folded paper figures make for elegant bookmarks (above). Variations on all these themes can be found throughout the Old Quarter, but particularly on Hang Ma, the street once dedicated to the art of paper and guild of paper craftsmen. Here you'll also find lots of vividly coloured lanterns, decorations and masks, all supremely light to pack and ideal as gifts to bring back home.

Khai Silk

This silk shop is Hanoi's most famous, and with good reason. Before founder Hoang Khai returned to traditional production techniques in the 1980s, the quality of Vietnamese silk had been poor, especially compared with imports, largely due to the years of conflict and an over-reliance on mechanisation. Khai, a graduate of the National Conservatory of Music, has since seen his business grow into the country's leading, and most expensive, silk-based fashion emporia, with boutiques in Hanoi and Ho Chi Minh City. Khai Silk's chic stores, designed by Khai, sell high-quality raw, taffeta and satin as accessories and ready-to-wear, but this is also the place to splurge on bespoke tailoring. By the time you get it home, it will seem like a bargain.
121 Ngo Nguyen Thai Hoc, T 747 0583, www.khaisilk-boutique.com

Pinocchio

The wooden sandal, usually made from the bead tree, is as Vietnamese as the conical hat, just less apparent to foreigners and Vietnam War film-makers. With the opening up of the country to capitalism, most Vietnamese switched to flip-flops or sneakers as their footwear of choice. Now, however, a number of boutiques in Hanoi are resurrecting the handmade wooden clog tradition. Pinocchio is one of the best, offering designs along the straps and lacquered soles inspired by scenes from *tuong* (traditional Vietnamese theatre). There are also more modern clogs in outlandish shapes and colours for those who want a conversation piece on their feet. The boutique also sells wood and silk bags and jewellery.
52 and 129 Hang Bong, T 928 7752, www.pinocchiovn.com

Marie-Linh Concept

Fashion designer Ho My Ha is better plugged in to contemporary tastes and more imaginative in her execution than most of her rivals – witness her chic linen blouses in black and Chinese red, which come with a side zipper. Outfits can be made to measure in linen, organza, cotton or raw silk.
74 Hang Trong, T 928 6304, www.marie-linh.com

Ý nguyện của Minh Ngọc luôn lấy chữ tín làm đầu để tránh sự nhầm lẫn với các hàng khác, Minh Ngọc lấy số 168 là ký hiệu riêng của mình. Quý khách tìm mua dùng hàng bánh chắc hẳn sẽ vui lòng với chất lượng Minh Ngọc 168. Hân hạnh phục vụ Quý khách.

海[
MINH NGO
BÁN

M[
NGO[

ĐẶC SẢN SỐ 1 HẢI DƯƠNG - VIỆT NA[
是南海阳市第一号特

Green bean cakes

These local delicacies can be found anywhere in the Far East that has been touched by Chinese culture – the city of Suzhou in Jiangsu, China, claims that it invented them. In Vietnam, that claim is made by the city of Hai Duong on the road from Hanoi to the sea, known locally as 'Green Bean Cake City'. At their most basic, they contain green bean paste and sugar, but can include ingredients such as sweet potato and coconut and rose oil. Either way, they are sold both in modern supermarkets, such as Trang Tien Plaza (24 Pho Hai Ba Trung), at street stalls and in smaller food stores, especially in the Old Quarter on Hang Gai. Some of the best are from the Rong Vang family firm, where they are handmade – look out for the name on the packaging (left). They are eaten all year round, but are tarted up for the Tet New Year celebrations.

SPORTS AND SPAS

WORK OUT, CHILL OUT OR JUST WATCH

Hanoians look after themselves pretty well – they might not surf, but they jog, play football and badminton and do tai chi. The footpaths around the lakes are crowded of a morning with panting yuppies, and there are many old folks under the trees doing their slow-mo ballet. In any odd corner of alley space or public park, someone will string up a badminton net and get a team game going of considerably more pace and interest than you will find in your average British provincial sports hall. Get yourself a good-value locally made racket on Trinh Hoai Duc and ask to join in. You'll be warmly welcomed – as long as you're not awful.

Football is huge here, and Vietnam's shared hosting of the 2007 AFC Asian Cup will only make it bigger. Check with your concierge for details of a local match, and if you're in luck with your timing, try to catch a game at the relatively new My Dinh National Stadium (see p092). The atmosphere at an international match is noisily enthusiastic but perfectly safe.

Golf is taking off like a three-wood tee shot, and the best course in northern Vietnam is about an hour out of town at Chi Linh Star (see p090). The clubhouse is a stunning circular structure on a hill overlooking two championship-standard courses. If it's something more sedentary you're after, book a treatment at Zen Spa (Thang Loi Hotel, Duong Yen Phu, T 719 9889), near the West Lake. *For full addresses, see Resources.*

Vuon Bach Thao

Designed by French landscape engineers in 1890, the Vuon Bach Thao is a 50-acre park behind the Presidential Palace of Vietnam. The state opened it to the public in 1954, and today it is filled with runners, footballers and tai chi practitioners. The easiest way to exercise with the locals is to join a badminton team game. Now, for some of us, badminton is a sport forever connected with a deeply unfashionable brand of 1970s Middle England leisure-centre culture, but in pockets of the Far East, it is a big deal, both at competition level and in the streets and parks. The best time to play is very early or in the evenings from 6 to 8pm. If you prefer the indoor version, you can try to get a game at the American Club (T 824 1850), but beware: the standard is very high.
Entrance on Duong Hoang Hoa Tham

Chi Linh Star Golf & Country Club
You've just got to love an exclusive club
that charges £12,000 per membership
yet still brazenly manages to incorporate
a red star in its logo. Irony is not a major
concept in Vietnam. Thankfully, non-
members can get a round for a much
more modest fee (£35 for 18 holes), but
make sure you book well in advance.
Sao Do, Chi Linh, Hai Duong,
T 4 771 9006, www.chilinhstargolf.com.vn

My Dinh National Stadium

Vietnamese football fans have a reputation for being the most dedicated, flag-waving, drum-beating and generally non-Confucian supporters in the Far East. Interest in the game has soared since a professional V-League was set up in 1980 and thanks to a run of good results by the national team. Arsenal has already set up a training academy in the country. However, it has to be said that while the fans are great, the Vietnamese players and officials have sadly often let them down by becoming embroiled in match-fixing scandals. Still, at least they have a nice stadium. My Dinh National Stadium was completed for the 2003 South East Asian Games and is a smart venue for 40,000 spectators. Bring a Vietnamese friend who can tell you if something dodgy is going on.

Hoa Lac

Sofitel Plaza pool and gym
There are plenty of good hotel gyms in
Hanoi, but probably the most dramatic
place to do your laps and workout is at
the Sofitel Plaza, thanks to its all-glass
Summit Lounge on the 20th floor. This
has breathtaking views across the West
Lake and Red River, and an all-weather
pool with a retractable roof.
*1 Duong Thanh Nien, T 823 8888,
www.sofitel-asia.com*

ESCAPES

WHERE TO GO IF YOU WANT TO LEAVE TOWN

Delightful as central Hanoi is, its immediate outskirts bear the scars of a hectic rush to progress after years of economic crisis. Visitors need to go a little further afield to escape the apartment blocks, light industry and highway strip development. Fortunately, there are some stunning experiences to be had once you make the break. Ha Long Bay (opposite) merits wonder-of-the-world hyperbole and its UNESCO designation. Its 2,000 limestone islands – most of them terrifyingly vertical and many pierced with grottos and caves – are a sight to behold. If you have time, the best way to appreciate the bay is to take a two- or three-day cruise. At least one night should be spent afloat, so you get the chance to wake up to the dawn mists that give the islands such an ethereal quality. You can sail in old-style luxury on the Emeraude – a beautiful colonial-style paddle steamer.

Other possible escapes include some beach time at the resorts dotted along the bay's edge, one of the finest being Tuan Chau Resort (Tuan Chau island, Quang Ninh, T 33 842 999), or a trip to the isolated northern hills, where ethnographic exploration can be combined with some serious pampering at the Victoria Sapa Resort (see p102). Alternatively, head south to central Vietnam and the luxurious Nam Hai resort (see p098). Take a day trip from here to explore the historic city of Hue.

For full addresses, see Resources.

Ha Long Bay

The mesmerising Ha Long Bay is northern Vietnam's top tourist draw and the pesky crowds of backpackers can be off-putting. The best way to rid yourself of them is to cruise the bay in a style they could not possibly afford. The gorgeous Emeraude is a replica of a 1910 paddle steamer that used to plough the coast hereabouts; only in those days the cargo wasn't well-heeled foreigners buzzed out on the tranquillity.

Nowadays, you can get a foot massage while drinking your sundowner – it's all polished wood floors, potted ferns, smiling service and frolicsomely fresh seafood buffets. And the view. If you can rouse yourself to some higher level of activity, the fake paddle lifts out of the water to provide a bathing platform.
Emeraude Classic Cruises, T 934 0888, www.emeraude-cruises.com

The Nam Hai

Rather than braving the treacherous and overcrowded Vietnamese roads, take the one-hour flight south to Da Nang, which is just 30 minutes from The Nam Hai resort (above and left). Every room has an unobstructed ocean view and all guests have access to 1km of private beach. When you've lazed in the sun long enough, head out to Hue, a two-hour drive away. Set on the banks of the Perfume River, this former imperial capital of the Nguyen dynasty is now a UNESCO World Heritage Site. Its walled citadel, with its ornately decorated gates (overleaf), and magnificent monuments and mausoleums remain largely intact, despite having been damaged in the 1968 Tet Offensive during the Vietnam War. *Hamlet 1, Dien Duong, Dien Ban, Quang Nam, T 510 940 000, www.thenamhai.com*

Eastern Gate, Hue

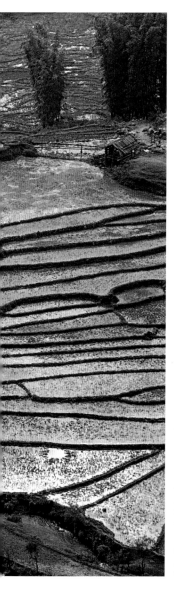

Victoria Sapa Resort

While in Hanoi, a visit to the northern mountains near the Chinese border is a must, but hours of Vietnamese pop blaring at you on a packed bus rather takes the sheen off the notion. Instead, why not let the train take the strain. And no ordinary train either: the ludicrously luxe Victoria Express transports guests of the Victoria Sapa Resort on a 10-hour trip through rice paddy fields (left) that you'll wish was longer. It has its own chef and two swooningly appointed wood-panelled sleeping carriages. The resort itself is a cosy upscale chalet affair from which you can tour local hill tribes or hire a mountain bike to explore neighbouring villages. Or you just could lounge about taking the air, sampling cuisine by the Parisian-trained chef and building up the energy for an acupressure massage.
Sapa, Lao Cai, T 20 871 522,
www.victoriahotels-asia.com

NOTES
SKETCHES AND MEMOS

RESOURCES
CITY GUIDE DIRECTORY

HOTELS
ADDRESSES AND ROOM RATES

Church Hotel 017
 Room rates:
 double, from $40;
 Superior Double, from $45
 9 Nha Tho
 T 928 8118
 www.churchhotel.com.vn

Daewoo Hotel 016
 Room rates:
 double, $150
 360 Pho Kim Ma
 T 831 5000
 www.hanoi-daewoohotel.com

Gia Bao Hotel 021
 Room rates:
 double, from $40;
 suite, from $45;
 Room 504, from $40;
 Suite 401, from $45;
 VIP 101, from $60;
 VIP 701, from $60
 38 Lo Su
 T 935 1494
 www.giabaohanoihotel.com

Hilton Hanoi Opera 022
 Room rates:
 double, $220
 1 Pho Le Thanh Tong
 T 933 0500
 www.hanoi.hilton.com

Meliá 023
 Room rates:
 double, $120;
 Executive Suite, $145
 44b Pho Ly Thuong Kiet
 T 934 3343
 www.meliahanoi.com

Sheraton Hotel 020
 Room rates:
 double, $200;
 Executive Suite, $460
 K5 Nghi Tam
 11 Xuan Dieu
 T 719 9000
 www.starwoodhotels.com

Sofitel Metropole 018
 Room rates:
 double, $330;
 Opera Suite, $590
 15 Ngo Quyen
 T 826 6919
 www.sofitel.com

Sofitel Plaza 016
 Room rates:
 double, $170
 1 Duong Thanh Nien
 T 823 8888
 www.sofitel.com

Thien Tan Hotel 017
 Room rates:
 double, $45
 12 Cha Ca
 T 824 4005
 www.thientanhotel.com

Zéphyr 016
 Room rates:
 double, from $90
 4 and 6 Pho Ba Trieu
 T 934 1256
 www.zephyrhotel.com.vn

WALLPAPER* CITY GUIDES

Editorial Director
Richard Cook

Art Director
Loran Stosskopf
City Editor
Sara Henrichs
Associate Writer
Paul McCann
Editor
Rachael Moloney
**Executive
Managing Editor**
Jessica Firmin

Chief Designer
Benjamin Blossom
Designer
Daniel Shrimpton
Map Illustrator
Russell Bell

Photography Editor
Christopher Lands
Photography Assistant
Robin Key

Chief Sub-Editor
Jeremy Case
Sub-Editors
Vicky McGinlay
Melanie Wells
Assistant Sub-Editor
Milly Nolan

Interns
Annaliese Bowell
Jemima Hills

**Wallpaper* Group
Editor-in-Chief**
Tony Chambers
Publishing Director
Andrew Black
Publisher
Neil Sumner

Contributors
Meirion Pritchard
Ellie Stathaki

Wallpaper* ® is a
registered trademark
of IPC Media Limited

All prices are correct at
time of going to press,
but are subject to change.

PHAIDON

Phaidon Press Limited
Regent's Wharf
All Saints Street
London N1 9PA

Phaidon Press Inc
180 Varick Street
New York, NY 10014

Phaidon® is a registered
trademark of Phaidon
Press Limited

www.phaidon.com

First published 2007
© 2007 IPC Media Limited

ISBN 978 0 7148 4741 2

A CIP Catalogue record for
this book is available from
the British Library.

All rights reserved.
No part of this publication
may be reproduced, stored
in a retrieval system or
transmitted, in any form
or by any means,
electronic, mechanical,
photocopying, recording
or otherwise, without
the prior permission of
Phaidon Press.

Printed in China

PHOTOGRAPHERS

Alexis Chabala
Foot badminton, p073
Paper doll, p081
Pinocchio, p083
Green bean cakes,
pp086-087

Marc Gerritsen
Hanoi city view, inside
front cover
Lenin statue, p012
Hanoi Opera House, p013
Temple of Literature,
pp014-015
Church Hotel, p017
Sofitel Metropole,
pp018-019
Gia Bao Hotel, p021
Hilton Hanoi Opera, p022
Meliá, p023
Les Comptoirs, p026
Ho Chi Minh Museum, p027
Green Tangerine,
pp030-031
Wild Lotus, p033
Press Club, pp034-035
Le Beaulieu, p036
Ly Club, p037
Bamboo Bar, pp038-039
I-Box, p040
Café Pho Co, p041
Vine Wine Boutique Bar
& Café, p042, p043

Solace, pp044-045
Hemispheres, p046
Emperor, p047
XY Café & Bar, pp048-049
Ba Mien, pp050-051
Bobby Chinn, pp052-053
Ha Linh Thu, p055
Hanoi Railway Station,
pp062-063
Hanoi Flag Tower, p064
Hanoi Towers, pp068-069
State Bank, pp070-071
Art Vietnam Gallery,
pp074-075
Ipa-Nima, p076, p077
Marena Hanoi, pp078-079
Le Vent, p080
Khai Silk, p082
Marie-Linh Concept,
pp084-085
Vuon Bach Thao, p089
My Dinh National Stadium,
pp092-093
Sofitel Plaza pool and gym,
pp094-095

**Robert Harding/
Digital Vision**
Eastern Gate, Hue,
pp100-101

**Bill Hatcher/
Getty Images**
Ha Long Bay, p097

Megapress/Alamy
Turtle Tower, p061

Compre Stephane/Alamy
Victoria Sapa Resort,
pp102-103

Joël Tettamanti
Ho Chi Minh Mausoleum,
pp010-011
Hoan Kiem, pp028-029
Long Bien Bridge, p060
Central Post Office, p065,
pp066-067

Andrew Woodley/Alamy
Hoan Kiem Lake, p025

HANOI
A COLOUR-CODED GUIDE TO THE HOT 'HOODS

TAY HO
The home of Hanoi's middle class and West Lake, laced with temples and pagodas

BA DINH
Brutalist builds meet French colonial villas in the country's administrative centre

THANH XUAN
Come here to see a show at the Water Puppet Theatre or skip town in a helicopter

HOAN KIEM
The city's beauty spot, Hoan Kiem Lake, is bordered by the bustling Old Quarter

HAI BA TRUNG
A pleasant residential zone featuring the pretty Lenin Park and Lien Phai Pagoda

CAU GIAY
Trek out to this neighbourhood for its museum, pagodas and delicious spring rolls

DONG DA
See the Soviet influence in Hanoi's architecture in buildings such as the railway station

TU LIEM
Venture here to watch a football match or tour the Hanoi National Convention Center

For a full description of each neighbourhood, see the Introduction.
Featured venues are colour-coded, according to the district in which they are located.